# Restored Too

# 2

## Rhonda Washington-Nelson

RH
RIVERHOUSE
PUBLISHING

MEMPHIS

## Restored Too

RiverHouse Publishing, LLC
1509 Madison Avenue
Memphis, TN 38104

All **RiverHouse Publishing, LLC** Titles, Imprints and Distributed Lines are available at special quantity discounts for bulk purchases for sales promotions, premiums, fund-raising and educational or institutional use.

First RiverHouse, LLC Trade Paperback Printing: 07/08/2017

**ISBN:  978-0-9988108-2-9**

Printed in the United States of America

This book is printed on acid-free paper.

**www.riverhousepublishingllc.com**

**To my children and grandchildren and to all the prayer warriors who fight daily on the front line.**

*Matthew 6: 33 ..."But seek ye first the kingdom of God, and his righteousness; and all these things shall be added unto you."* (King James Version)

# Insert

Ayala cherished the compound. It was the place she called home. Under the protective eye of her mistress, master, and mama, Ayala knew she was fortunate to reside in a place where her spirit could roam free. While it required hard work from all the maidens and servants who lived within this camp, Ayala could think of no other place she would rather be. Her master, whom she revered, was an extremely prosperous man and ran a household filled with warmth and gaiety. Ayala's master and mistress were blessed with ten rowdy children whom they both adored very much. As a young girl, Ayala loved the excitement the master's wild brood generated whenever they visited their parents—which by the way, was often.

It was one fateful day, however, that a dark cloud descended upon the compound—instantly snatching away all of her master's earthly possessions. Shortly thereafter, matters went from bad to worse when a mysterious illness overtook his body and all ten of his children were killed by a fierce whirlwind.

Devastated by life's traumatic events, his wife was left to fend for the family. Along with bearing the burden of maintaining the compound, mistress was also slowly dying with grief. Mourning the loss of her precious children, the weight of her trials grew insurmountable. In a moment of weakness

Ayala's mistress uttered a few ill-fated words to her husband that wreaked havoc in each of their lives, seemingly forever. *"Curse God and die"* was the language that deepened the divide between husband and wife and caused life-changing conditions to occur within the compound. If only mistress could have taken the blasphemous words back would soon be all of their desires.

Irretrievable,—the words caused hopelessness to follow them where ever they went.

Yet, despite the desperation all around, Ayala refused to yield to the cold hand of despair. From a secret place, she found God and gained revelation into who He was and what He alone could do. Formulating a relationship with God that produced life-sustaining faith and unshakable trust, Ayala grew into a young woman of deep spiritual conviction.

While the ferocious whirlwind and illness generated them a devastating blow, it was those same calamities that offered them revelation into the sovereignty of God and the true meaning behind tests and trials.

Forging victoriously through hardship and tribulations, it was not only Ayala's master who was restored in the end—by the grace of God......they all were.

# Chapter One

My name is Ayala.

Many around the compound where I live refer to me as '*YaYa*. I am not too fond of the nickname, but as years have passed, I have grown accustomed to it.

I guess it's a step-up from my younger years when everyone called me, '*Yas*.

Now, that was a name I could live without! I re-membered praying real hard one day that everyone would just stop calling me that and simply refer to me as Ayala.

It partially worked. Shortly after that, '*YaYa* emerged.

So, for right now, '*YaYa* it is!

While these are all loving and endearing titles, I have learned one thing—it's only one manner in which I am called that truly matters.

Pronouncing each syllable, "A(Ah)-ya-la", my mother's smooth, strong, voice can be heard from miles around ringing out my name. No one else calls me quite like she does. Whenever she cries out like that, it causes me to stop in my tracks. Where ever I am and whatever I'm doing, nothing is more im-portant than going to see what mama has on her mind for me to do.

My mother is an amazing woman.

I guess speaking like a-proud-only-child, no one could ask for a more caring, loving, and ridiculously smarter parent than mine. Even the women and younger girls around the compound take to her like a magnet. Time after time, I'll watch them seek mama's sound and wise advice. These women are willing—literally, to stand in line for hours just to talk to her in order to ease their troubled minds. My mother has the innate ability of comforting each one of them, offering them the solace their weary souls desperately need. Besides being an exceptional listener, mama has a skill that I must admit stumps even my most critical and rational thinking. It's a unique gift of hers that I have the privilege alone of dealing with and trying hard to understand. It goes like this...where ever and whatever I am doing, mama can track my coming and going—almost stealth-like; at all times. When I find myself deep in my own thoughts and tending to my secretive affairs, mama calls out for me. It's as if she knows what I am about to do and stops me before I venture too far into potential trouble. How she does that simply blows my mind! Each year, I vow to figure out exactly what causes that gut reaction of hers to kick in, and each year, I fail. In fact, mama seems to get a whole lot better at tracking my whereabouts faster than I am at figuring out how she keeps up with me so well.

I guess this somewhat clairvoyant tendency of hers was the reason my legs now shook like it was well-below freezing outside. I was expecting at any moment for my mother to call out my name.

You see, it was the third instance I peeked through the lattice into the room they had forbidden me in. They warned me several times to stay away, but the first time I heard them say, "Bear down child!" I couldn't resist.

"Ayala!" my mother finally cried out to me.

I jumped at the sound of my name being called. It frightened me so until I wanted to dash straight for the bathroom before entering to see what it was she wanted.

"Yes ma'am, here I am," I said rushing in. The innocent look I portrayed was in hopes of disguising my disobedience.

"Quick, run and tell master, we are going to the stone."

*Going to the stone*…. Well, I knew exactly what that meant.

Like a beam from a reflective light, I tore through the door out onto the wide opened plain. My legs carried me faster than the wind as I kicked up a trail of dust behind me. Like my name, which I am told means "gazelle", I raced with the gracefulness and swiftness of one.

"My lord!" I said, bowing to the earth when I finally reached him.

Mounted high upon the beautiful, black stallion he so often rode, he looked out at me.

"Our mistress has taken to the stone," I said panting, rapidly breathing in the crisp mountain air.

I watched as master turned away; then, slowly, effortlessly, gaze up at the hilly terrain that had now become his friend. As if there were untold secrets between the two of them, he stared for a moment, his thoughts thoroughly consumed by the curvaceous hills and valleys. I knew what had him captivated and rendered him so speechless. Still, I stood quietly beside master until the silent conversation between he and the place he had grown to love—the mountainous territory, ceased.

"I am on my way!" he finally called out to me, pulling the reigns tightly to the dazzling mare. Patting his prized horse, he faced the main house and stared.

I bowed again and like a flash tore off towards the compound hoping I had not missed the finale. As fast as my legs would carry me, I ran. With the wind at my back giving me the extra momentum I needed, I slowed momentarily when I heard the cries of a newborn infant piercing the air.

"It's a boy!" the ladies yelled out.

By the time I reached the courtyard, I was confronted with a mass of joyful women who seemed to have appeared from every region of Uz, dancing, crying and embracing one another in excitement!

I ran straight towards the large-wooden frame that had been my protection in the past. It was the front-row seat that afforded me the opportunity to witness the beautiful baby boy being softly cuddled in my mistress' arms. Swept up by the intimate scene—all of my emotions exploded inside as a steady flow of tears rushed my eyes.

It was master's entrance that reeled in my thoughts and feelings.

For the first time in several years, I witnessed him being introduced to his first living son.

# Chapter Two

Even though I was too young to recall all the happier times, I do remember when master's eldest son and his six handsome brothers came to visit. There was always food galore and plenty of noise and chatter. They were somewhat of a rowdy crew and whenever all seven boys and three girls got together, I found myself staying up half the night listening in on their wild and elaborate tales. I was convinced master's daughters were equally amusing as his sons, the only difference being—they had the task of preparing fine meals for all to enjoy. Whenever the girls came to celebrate, they always took over the food preparation duties from the household maidens ordinarily assigned those chores.

The dining area became chaotic whenever these girls were around. I'm sure their motto was, "the messier, the better".

"Look, you've got flour in your hair," I recalled one of the daughter's squeal to the other.

"Yes, and you put it there," the other shot back, throwing a fist-full of the white-powdery substance her way.

"Oh, no you did not," the powdered-covered victim would cry out.

Now, that is when the first of the food-fights would begin. Leeks, figs, grapes and flour were tossed back and forth.

When it was all over, a haze of white fog permeated the air causing us all to cough and gag our heads off as we tried fanning away the fumes. The rest of the maidens and I took cover under tables or any place else we could find refuge. We all stared in disbelief as the daughters screamed and laughed in delight. This happy brood was quite a handful.

My eyes grew large when I suddenly became aware of the tall, robust figure, standing in the doorway to inquire of the commotion.

It was master.

His daughters quickly grabbed anything they could that gave the semblance of being busy—pretending to be hard at work putting together the meal they had originally been assigned.

Waving the air, trying to remove any hint of the flour-fighting contest, one would grab the broom sweeping away the evidence, while the other quickly wiped down the stone counters. The third daughter, peeking into the pot of stew as if concerned about its progress.....all three making it appear to be preoccupied with their duties while suppressing the laughter threatening to spill its way out.

Shaking his head from side to side, master would slowly remove himself from the scene, and when he did, peals of laughter would burst forth as each proclaimed to be the victor.

It was all quite a sight to behold and I loved every minute of it!

I had overheard the servant girls complain one day about the master's daughters' rambunctious

ways to each other, but they dared not let on to anyone else that it bothered them so.

"They make such a mess of everything," they said.
"Then we are left to clean up after them.  It takes us
days to get the place back in order the way our mistress likes it," the maidens would complain.

As for me, I did not mind the intrusion at all.  In
fact, I was the happiest when the girls were
around—having to run numerous errands for them
throughout the day.

It was during the daughter's visits that I would
put my sprinting skills to use.  Off I would run to fetch
whatever the younger ladies asked me for.  When I
would finally return from one of my many trips, I re-
membered realizing how quickly the home had
transformed itself into a bustling yet festive place to
be.  The gaiety and celebration inside was infectious,
and often lasted for days.

One afternoon, in my secret location, I overheard
a conversation between master, and his eldest son
taking place.

"Take it to your house," I heard master say.  "The
elders from the surrounding towns are visiting more
often than I had anticipated and our business affairs
are increasing.  It does warm my heart, however, to
see just how much you, your brothers and sisters
truly enjoy each other," he said.

I watched as master belt out that hearty laugh of
his.

"It is what I have worked so hard for. It is how
family should be, but the gatherings must now take
place in your own home, son."

"*No...,*" I wanted to cry out. How was I ever going to find out what happened to master Laban's goats—crazy stories like that if they took the parties away?

"Don't worry father," his eldest son said, gently holding onto master's arm. "It will be an honor to host the next celebration. In fact, I am looking forward to it. The day will be one filled with enjoyment and delight—it is the day that you were born. We shall all rejoice!"

"*Oh, no,*"...it was an even greater disappointment. It was master's birthday!

Ever since I could remember, I had been around to witness the crowds of people who made their way to the compound on that day. Men of notoriety came bearing luxurious gifts along with many well-deserved accolades to shower upon master. Year after year, these notable men from afar made their way to his birthday celebration and would abide in the compound for days. During that time, I got a chance to see how these important men and their beautiful wives interacted with one another. Dressed in the finest apparel, I was always captivated by the strange yet regal way our master and mistress spoke and flowed among their fellow guests.

You see.... dreaming so often about the aristocratic lifestyle ignited a fire so intense inside of me—I have never been able to extinguish it. That same fire seared a hole deep within, causing me to long for the days I would experience that same dignity, wealth, and class, just like these fine folk did.

When the distinguished callers arrived, I never knew which secret place I wanted to visit the most.

I guess you can tell by now, exploring the compound was one of my favorite past-time activities. I have found crevasses and secret hide-a-ways inside and outside the home that I am sure no one else knows exist. It was as if whoever built the compound did it with my explorations and adventurous nature in mind. Carving out the perfect spots to be able to see and hear exactly what was going on without being seen—these secluded caverns gave me access to a world overflowing with fun-filled discoveries and all kinds of information.

So, whenever the galas would take place, I made multiple trips... bouncing between the secret places, listening in on the men—especially when they were well drunken with wine... telling tales even greater than the ones master's sons told. Then back to the women I would go, completely absorbed by their conversation as they spoke of very personal matters.

During this time of celebration, every space in the house was taken up by master's guests. Even mama and I were displaced for a while having to lodge in the other servants' sleeping quarters so the important entourage could have somewhere comfortable to reside.

It never bothered me at all being temporarily moved like that. As long as my mother was by my side, I was content. Besides, I have learned, where ever I go, there are always adventures to be made— conversations to listen to—and places to explore.

\*\*\*

After the shock subsided of master's request to his son, I was immediately drawn back into the conversation between the two.

"I will see you in a few weeks at my home for the great celebration," the eldest son exclaimed.

I watched as he and his father smiled and warmly embraced.

Before exiting the room, the young man reached over and lightly kissed his mother on the cheek.

Mistress gently reached up to stroke her son's face.

It was the last time I recalled her ever seeing her first born alive again.

# Chapter Three

The darkness quickly descended upon the once festive home, dimming its light seemingly forever. It was that fateful day when I spotted the servant in the distance rushing towards the compound—eyes wide and haunted. I knew something was dreadfully wrong as soon as he pushed open the gate. His clothes seemingly scorched and tattered, the frayed courier fell upon the earth as he entered the bustling courtyard. Forcing himself up, he crept to the table where master sat.

Running to my secret place, I arrived just in time to hear him tell master the disastrous news. I barely had time to comprehend what had just occurred when several other servants arrived, telling different accounts of more heart-wrenching tragedies.

All ten were dead.

It was those words that muted the world around me. A few seconds ticked by and I could no longer hear the bleating of the sheep... nor feel the moist, cool breeze blowing against my skin. There was no sound coming from the mouth of the servant telling the story or those screaming in horror. Rendered deaf for a moment, the words he spewed out left me staggering. Even my lungs refused to cooperate as I longed for the fresh air to fill them again.

Suddenly, the mechanism that triggered my breathing kicked in and the rhythm controlling my lungs worked like before. When time finally caught up with my emotions, I remembered clenching my mouth so hard that it left a mark on my upper lip. I did all I could to suppress the scream threatening to spill its way out. Careful not to expose my secret hide-away, I stood quietly, groped by fear and shock as it spread itself violently throughout my small body.

Finally, I looked up at the culprits who had just caused all of our distress. It was the dark, ominous clouds looming overhead that had formed the whirlwind and was now staring down angrily at me. The twister forming clouds were unrelenting and deadly, and didn't seem to care who the unfortunate victims were that crossed their paths.

As I recall, the winds had been blowing ferociously all day long—the sky black as midnight. Whenever that happened, I always stayed close by my mother's side. It was the animal's behavior, however, that gave me the premonition a great storm was on the horizon. No matter how hard the servants tried, those responsible for the herd could not settle them.

When the tornadic winds tore through the compound with such tremendous force, I knew this storm was a different one. I shivered whenever I recalled the wind-gusts' sounds—howling like hundreds of jackals on a restless summer night, underneath a full-moon. Banging violently against the windows and doors, the fierce winds caused the earth to shake beneath me.

Fearing any moment the whirlwind would whisk me up into its deadly grasp, I held on tightly as it passed us by. Roaring like the vibration of hundreds of bullocks trampling the wide-open plains, I covered my ears and prayed.

The only thing offering me any degree of consolation was the tranquil look upon my mother's face. Even in the midst of the most tempestuous storm, she never showed fear. I watched her smile and then gently close her eyes, and whisper over and over again, "Our God is a great protector in every storm....."

Once the fury of the tumultuous tempest moved on, its aftermath gave us all plenty of tasks to perform. The force of the wind lifted the tops from most of the animal's stalls. The men were fast at work repairing the damaged sheds while the women gathered the strewn about utensils, tools, and clothing sprinkled like confetti throughout the yard. It was during that time that I noticed the servant running towards the compound carrying the dreadful news of master and mistress' deceased children.

The whirlwind had torn straight through the eldest son's house where all ten of master's children were gathered. It left nothing standing.

When the gasping boy reached his final destination and reported the news, it was master's wail that etched an everlasting scar now firmly planted in my memory. His long screech shook the ground and the vibrations from it could be felt for miles around. The strange sound seemed to come from a depth so deep, it caused me to recoil in fright.

Watching a man of insurmountable strength succumbing to a moment of such death-defying pain was incomprehensible to me. Nothing had ever prepared me to grapple with the inexplicable sound of grief and anguish coming from a man of such great power. I understood the magnitude of his traumatic heartache and knew it would impact his life forever.

No one could ever be prepared to hear the news—there were no survivors.

That night in bed, I could hear mistress' shrill screams too, rumbling through the air, like billows of angry waters dashing hard against the rocks. The sound reached all the way to where I hid underneath the covers.

"Ahhhhh, it cannot be," mistress cried out over and over again.

As sleep eluded the grief-stricken mother, I heard her call to each of her children as if they were somewhere close by listening.

When covering my ears no longer muffled the agonizing sound, I crept in bed with my mother to escape the frightful shrieks.

Even as a young girl, I understood I would never-ever forget this very dark night—the time when everything changed.

# Chapter Four

The shadows of darkness lingered as the funerals for all ten children took place. Mama forced me to stay at home, but from the secret place, I could see each of their faces before they departed. Master walked around with an unusual—eerie quietness from room to room. Even from where I sat, he seemed strikingly thin. My beautiful mistress no longer resembled the regal woman I had grown accustomed to, but ambled behind her husband as they left for the burials.

With the assistance of the older maidens and servants, withdrawn and haggard, mistress and master trailed all ten biers. I watched as the endless line of mourners left the compound sobbing as they marched their way up the rocky hill.

While I stood there gazing, not a muscle of mine decided it wanted to move. Frozen in place, I watched until the last of the crowd passed out of sight. I felt the pounding of my heart beating hard inside, rocking the rest of my body in rhythmic fashion. I was in no way prepared to deal with people carrying boxes of those I had grown to know and love encased inside.

Bending over, I threw-up the food I had managed to eat.

Mama had given me a list of chores to finish, hoping perhaps to keep me busy and take my mind away from the harsh reality I was forced to face. However, my own grief now consumed me and household tasks was the last thing I wanted to deal with. Still, I completed most of my duties, but felt an overwhelming sense of tiredness as I set about tending to the last few. The moment they were all finally done, I curled up in my favorite blanket and waited.

Hours later, when I spied the first of the women dressed in black coming towards the compound, I headed out to greet them.

Then, I hesitated.

Understanding the gravity of the day,—I decided to remain where I was.

Finally, I spotted mama. I watched as the tall, graceful woman walked the long dusty road alone. Entering the gates of the compound, it was only then that I ventured outside walking slowly up to her. The moment we embraced... a mutual sense of relief and comfort flowed between the two us. We both understood we would never-ever take for granted the privilege of being able to hold onto someone whom we truly loved. As we clung tightly to each other— for a brief instance, I felt safe again.

For the rest of the day, I followed mama everywhere she went. Soon we joined the other ladies in preparing food for all those attending the somber, grief-stricken occasion.

It was obvious many of the women had the same thing in mind. Gathering in a safe place like the dining area somehow eased our minds and gave us a place to discuss sensitive matters openly without fear of reprisal.

The atmosphere seemed different now. The mood was as if it foretold of gloomier days ahead. It caused my stomach to tighten—my throat parched. It did not make matters any better when I heard the other servants whispering to one another.

"Our mistress will not eat a thing," one of the younger maidens said, as we all busied ourselves preparing dishes for the guest.

"It has been three days and not a morsel has she placed in her mouth," the other maiden offered.

Without a word being spoken, I watched as those gathered in the room—communicating only with their eyes, turn and stare at mama.

My mother ignored them.

"Maybe you can get her to take in a few crumbs," the young brave maiden finally spoke up. Facing mama now, she continued her challenge. "You have always been her favorite. She will do whatever you ask. You were there when all ten of her children were born. You are special to her."

Not one word parted mama's lips as she scurried about the dining area.

In fact, I noticed just how little mama had to say these past few days. I watched as she reached over and stoked the hearth as the uncomfortable silence overshadowed the room.

Then, out of nowhere….suddenly, mama's voice shattered the quietness.

"She will be okay, our mistress is still young," she forced out while kneading the dough with her nimble fingers. "It is my lord that I am mostly concerned about. He does not appear well and the grief is only making matters worse."

"What will he do with each of us?" the other young lady whispered. "How can he afford to sustain everybody now? He's lost everything. We will all starve."

"Hush, now," mama said. "Not in front of the child."

Despite all that was happening, mama never dropped her guard. When it came to me, she was always protective.

However, this time the young maiden ignored her request and persisted on. "There is a rumor that master was trying to get a group together to fight the Sabeans who stole the herd and killed our friends." Lowering her voice even further, the servant-girl whispered, "I also heard no one was willing to go with him to battle."

"Enough," mama cried out strong and loud.

Silence quickly filled the air again. Only an occasional request for a food item could be heard after that.

The quietness made space for the unthinkable trauma that had victimized each one of us in the room, forcing the sad events of the day to once again come into the forefronts of our minds.

I am sure everyone was thinking about no longer hearing the silly tales the young men told. Most of all, no more food fights from the beautiful girls. Instead, all ten children were somewhere neatly buried out there on a rocky hillside.

Many of the young maidens in the dining area dabbed their eyes periodically as they went about tending to their specific culinary duties. One young maiden tried to lighten the mood, and entertain us in conversation about her trip to the market that day. When no one responded, she too resigned herself to silence.

There had never been a time when I could recall feeling so afraid. The gloomy, foreboding shadow of fear followed me everywhere I went. I think it was mostly because I had witnessed my mama crying. I had never seen her weep like that before. With eyes now droopy and reddened, I watched as she quietly reached into her apron's pocket and pull out the handkerchief she had tucked inside. Lifting the decorative linen cloth to her eyes, she wiped the tears that gently cascaded their way down her cheeks.

When I crawled in bed with mama that night, I tried my best to comfort her as I held her tightly.

# Chapter Five

The rumors were true.  Several of the maidens and their families left the compound as soon as the food supply became scarce.

The compound was a very different place now.

Mama was placed in charge of food rationing. She was also responsible for redistributing the work load as the servants began leaving the compound one by one.

Master had not been outside the home in months and his appearance had become increasingly unrecognizable—even to me.  His frail looks gave me a great sense of pain and sadness.  Here I was witnessing a man I had grown to admire, succumb to an unexplainable illness, and face tragedies that surpassed human limitations.

Each day I tried to seek out the man I once knew—only to leave disappointed.

I always thought I would marry a man much like master... someone rich, handsome, and who took care of his wife in a loving yet regal manner.  The man I would spend the rest of my life with would be able to afford the elegant apparel I'd wear, just like mistress.  There would be times of course where I would assist him in his business affairs—as much as I could.  Mostly, I would run an efficient and happy household the way mistress so effortlessly did. Master always seemed extremely pleased with how his wife handled it all.

It was the dramatic change in master and mistress' behavior that caused me to re-think my dreams, however. Their sullen demeanor and attitude had somehow drawn the life, dreams and hopes out of all of us.

I knew despite all the trauma both of them now faced, they still truly loved each other.

It was mama who told me the bedtime stories of how the master's and mistress' paths first crossed.

"She was barely fifteen years old when they met," mama explained.

"Both were fortunate to come from well-to-do families and at the tender young age of sixteen, she became his bride. During the wedding festivities, the décor around the compound was so amazing Ayala, you could see the sparkle the candles made from miles away," mama would boast.

"The women all came adorned in their beautiful, expensive decorative gowns, but none of them compared to mistress. She was fairer than even our beautiful matriarch Sarah I have told you so much about. She was lovelier than anything you could have imagined," mama exclaimed.

"Oh, how I wish I was there to witness the beautiful sight. Describe it all again," I pleaded.

"Okay, okay. After months of preparation, her complexion glowed like that of a newly hewn marble with a gloss so captivating our master knew he was a lucky man," mama laughed.

"Her wavy locks were so dark that the fine gold and pearls intertwined between the flowing tresses shimmered like stars on a crisp-starry night. The gown was meticulously sewn and had to be carefully guarded in order to protect the precious jewels the family had given to be placed upon it. Handcrafted by those who were gifted to create such a master-piece, the dress fit her to perfection. The unveiling of the bride—adorn in great splendor, was the high-light of the entire ceremony. Mistress was so stun-ning, Ayala, words seemed to fail our master," mama said.

"I have never seen him so proud and well.....so speechless," mama laughed.

"The celebration lasted for days."

"Oh, how I wish I could have been there," I re-membered squealing.

From the time I could recall, all I had ever known was the unconditional love and respect these two beautiful people showered upon each other. No one could have convinced me that the love master and mistress shared was not the purest and truest in the whole wide world. I frequently watched from my secret place how master would gently caress mis-tress' face with his hands before he parted for the day's work. After all the years I had been living on the compound, I still witnessed them gazing softly into each other's eyes, very much like first-time lov-ers. Whenever they had their grand affairs, master would swirl mistress around as if they were the only two present in the entire room. I was convinced it was that same love that made mama and me feel so warmly welcomed like family all these years.

"Was my father at the wedding mama?" I asked softly.

"Yes, he was, Ayala, and it was one of the happiest times for your father and me that I can remember."

~~

My thoughts abounded as I stared into the distance.

Hearing stories like that somehow increased the sadness I felt.

I wanted...I longed so much for a sliver of those trouble-free, care-free days prior to the traumas.

Now, things were no longer the same—my thoughts shifting back to the dismal reality. Two uninvited guests called hopelessness and despair had forced their way into each of our lives and refused to leave.

Master rarely came out of his bed-chambers and mistress seldom went in.

Neither mama nor I had officially seen master in quite some time. Unlike the instances when we would occasionally bump into him during those happier times, master now found himself sadly confined to the cramped living space of his bedroom.

The only time I saw mistress enter into their sleeping quarters recently was to take him the special balm mama made for his wounds.

However, today was one of those days mistress decided to pay him a visit.

Stretching to hear a little better from my secret place near the open window, I listened as mistress walked into their bedroom. I could barely hear what they said to each other as master spoke softly to his wife.

Sneaking a look inside, I caught a glimpse of master as he shuffled towards the broken pot set aside in his room. Picking up a sharp edge of the pottery, I watched him slowly—painfully began to scrape his marred skin. Withdrawing in horror, I turned away when the stream of blood oozed from each of the dark-crusted wounds.

The sight I witnessed was way beyond anything I had ever seen before. It was master talking, but his frail, infested, shell of a body, covered with hideous sores and scabs was not the man that matched the voice. I reached deep down inside to keep the small amount of food I had just digested from coming up. After taking several deep breaths, the nausea soon subsided.

From my secret spot, I watched as mistress slowly emerged from the room, gently closing the door behind her. Standing there momentarily, I looked upon the weary-eyed, fatigued woman, silently weeping, all alone. Holding an arm full of sheets that seemed soiled beyond ever being cleaned again, I followed mistress as she slowly walked to the back of the house, placing each of the filthy bedwear into the boiling pot of water.

Utilizing the poker iron to push her husband's bed linen inside, she jumped and screamed as the stinging droplets of water fell upon her arm.

Dropping the rest of the linen, she ran to the compound's well, placing the scalded area deep into the soothing water.

It seemed mistress remained there for hours.

I finally conceded that things were even worse than I imagined.  I had never seen mistress perform domestic tasks like the ones she was taking on now.  I was keenly aware no one else was there to fulfill these duties since most of the servants had long vacated the premises, so she had to pick up the slack.

I looked on as mistress finally withdrew her arm from out of the cool water.  A noticeable angry, reddened area pulsated as she cried out in agony.

I recalled those sheets remaining on the ground for several months after that.

Later, during the night as I lay in bed finding it difficult to sleep, I heard a faint knock on our bungalow's door.

"Who's there?" mama called out.

"It's me," the soft voice replied.

Easing out of bed, mama slowly released the latch.

It was mistress, clutching her wrap—shielding herself from the cool night air.

"May we talk?" I heard mistress ask.

Reaching for her cloak and wrapping herself inside, I watched as mama exit the room.

Immediately jumping out of bed and falling onto my knees, I pressed my eye against the tiny hole that had been in the door for as long as I could remember.  I stared hard at the two ladies as they sat on the steps of the porch to our living quarters.

The intense look on mama's face while she examined the reddened blistered area seeming to cover mistress' forearm, spoke of the rare instance I had ever seen her worry.

"Let me get you something to put on that," mama said.

When she opened the door to our room, I laid as still as possible pretending to be asleep.

I'd almost gotten caught when she abruptly came back into the room like that. As soon as mama left again, I slipped out of bed and listened in on the conversation between the two women.

"Why couldn't I have died too?" mistress asked. She cried out in pain as mama tended to the wound.

"Oh-h-h," she winced pulling her arm away. "Why is this happening to me? I do not understand! I have asked God what I did that was so wrong. I have already asked Him for forgiveness just in case there is anything. This is beyond what I am able to bear and I don't know what to do!" she sobbed.

I watched mama gently reach for mistress again. Hugging her, mama looked sympathetically into her eyes.

"There is no doubt my husband has been kind to everyone," mistress continued. "He is such a good man," she whimpered. "I have never once heard him say a harsh word to anyone, even when I knew they deserved it. If you ask me, he was kind almost to a fault ....helping all those people who came seeking assistance. Often times, I felt they took advantage of his generosity and kindness," mistress explained, placing the napkin to her tear stained face.

"No matter how hard I tried, I could never talk him out of helping any of the people who sought relief. It is just like I thought though, now that he is suffering, no one is here to comfort him," mistress said. Pausing for a brief moment she buried her face in her hands and wept.

"It seems even God has turned His back on him," she cried out loud. "I can see the light slowly fading from his eyes."

She looked up at mama. "He is giving up!" she sobbed. "If he dies, there will be nothing left of me. I love him so much that I may as well find a grave for myself too," she yelled defiantly. "Besides, I have no sons to care for me. I have nothing worth living for," she cried.

Even from where I knelt, I could see the redness and dark circles that buried themselves deep beneath mistress' eyes.

"We will ask God for help," mama said.

I didn't hear mama say much of anything else after that, but through the small opening, I watched as she offered the type of support she was well known for.

Mama prayed.

I eased my way back in bed as the conversation continued into the early hours of the morning.

When mama finally returned, even though I didn't want it to be so....I could tell she had been crying.

# Chapter Six

The sunlight streamed its way through the thin curtains. It was the soft tap on my shoulder that caused me to stir.

"We have so many chores to complete today, Ayala," mama whispered in my ear. "Let us try and get a head start on them. Come and eat my little one."

I eased out of bed and poured the warm water she had prepared for me into the basin as I washed and dressed, then hurried outside.

Once inside the dining area, I enjoyed the refreshing taste of a few figs, a small slice of barley bread with melted cheese, and milk.

Mama managed to have a hearty meal prepared for all of us even though the food was scare.

"Ayala, as soon as you finish your breakfast, please go and find mistress and offer her your assistance," mama called out.

"Yes ma'am."

Later, when I found mistress washing linen, sheets and other assortments of clothing, I jumped in to help. It took some adjustment at first, but I was beginning to get used to the more strenuous household duties. In fact, I actually enjoyed the small tips mistress gave me on how to perform particular tasks just the right way. It seemed mistress was becoming more accustomed to all the work the compound required. Every now and then, I would even witness a hint of a smile whenever she went about performing chores that had special meaning to her.

Still, no matter how hard mama and I tried, nothing ignited that special spark mistress used to radiate when all of her children were alive.

After the clothes were hung to dry, mama, mistress, and I were busy in the garden securing ingredients for our afternoon meal.

I picked several of the plump ears of corn that were still available. I also found a few large potatoes for the stew.

I could not help but wonder what would happen when the food ran out. The thought lingered in the back of my mind causing a gnawing in my stomach to occur that just would not go away.

I continued gathering the produce and prayed continuously that things would soon return back to normal.

Reality quickly slipped its way back in when we all gathered in the dining area to prepare the meal. It was there where I noticed how extremely thin mistress had become. The moment she bent over the open hearth to stir the brewing stew, her protruding shoulder blades were so evident it made her neck and face appear skeletal-like. The color in mistress' once vibrant cheeks no longer existed. The scowl that formed the "V" in her brow seemed permanently etched there now.

Trauma and grief took full advantage of the mistress of the house, and these two felons were determined to win at all cost.

No matter how hard I prayed, I knew in my heart things were not getting any better. It was the long talks at night between mistress and mama that told me so. Conversing on the steps had become their night time ritual. It had also become a part of my daily routine to eavesdrop on the troubling conversation between the two women.

Mistress posed the same question—night after night.

"Why did God have to take all of them?" she cried out into the brisk night air. "We may as well have lived unclean lives if this is how we were going to end up," she lamented.

I remember one night in particular when the discussion between mama and mistress took a sudden, even darker turn.

Tiredness wore on mistress like a multi-layered quilt. The words she spoke next, matched her weariness.

"He is no longer the man I married."

It was the lack of emotion in mistress' voice that caused me to shiver. Cold and impersonal,—she spoke on.

"He pushes me away and absolutely hates when I come around. I don't say much to him anymore," she told mama. "It has been like that for months now. I guess he has fallen out of love with me. I have even considered going back home to my father's house," she whispered. "My fear is, only destruction awaits us here."

Mistress then shook her head as if to gather herself—trying to settle her thoughts.

"If I am going to keep the compound afloat, I must figure out how to pay the taxes they are calling for. I cannot keep avoiding the men who are asking for them."

Pausing for a moment, she faced mama, "I do not know why you stay here with me. Take *'YaYa* and go. She is a goodly child. She will marry well one day and take care of you. As for me, I have nothing to look forward to but the friendly hand of death—whose grasp I feel obliged to firmly hold."

Noticing how the tears intersected beneath mistress' chin, I watched as she stared into mama's eyes, and then warmly embraced her.

"Thank you for your loyalty," mistress said. "You know....you have always been more than just a maiden in this household." She spoke softly, "You truly are my friend."

I held my breath as I awaited mama's response. Had mistress just suggested we leave the compound? Had I heard that right? Was that even an option?

I finally let out a great sigh of relief when I heard mama speak.

"Is there any place we can go where my daughter and I could experience the kind of graciousness and love you and master have extended to us these many years?" mama asked.

I watched as mama glanced away, staring into the darkness,—drenched in the warmth of her fondest memories.

She spoke softly, "After Ayala's father passed away, I did not know what would happen to us or where we would go," she admitted. "How could I ever forget that cold and miserable night? It was the most alone and helpless I have ever felt. It was, however, that same night that you and master came to see about me. Do you remember how the both of you reassured me I had nothing to fear? You promised that Ayala and I would always be taken care of. The proof was not just in your words, mistress, your actions have spoken for you ever since that day," mama said. "I have never had the opportunity to thank you for all that you and master have done for us these many years like I wanted to. Ayala has been healthy and happy, and for that I am truly grateful. Now, that God has given me the opportunity to repay you for all your kindness,—I will do everything in my power to do just that. The compound is our home, and Ayala and I are not going anywhere. We are family and family will always stick together."

The tears clouded mistress' eyes.

I slipped away quietly and curled up in bed. For the first time, tranquility and hope had eased its way back into my troubled mind.

Suddenly, I realized how proud I was of mama, mistress and master.

I closed my eyes and for a long time, unlike past nights, I slept soundly.

I was home. I was with family.

# Chapter Seven

I loved to hear mama tell the story of how we ended up in this beautiful part of the country. It all began when I started asking questions about my father. I guess at this point mama felt I was old enough to understand. So, she told me all about our own personal tragedy and exactly what happened to my father.

It was one night when we cozied by the fire in the bungalow that mama decided she was going to tell me everything about how my father died. I guess considering the present set of circumstances, she felt the need to.

This time, she left nothing out.

"Your father had been a wonderful husband to me and was overseer of the very compound we now live in," she started out. "He was a faithful steward to our current master's father who entrusted him with all of his affairs. They called master's father, Abir. I am told he was strong, and kind, just like master," mama said.

"As a young man, your father grew up with master and they shared a bond akin to brothers. When master's father unexpectedly passed away and left him all of his possessions, your father continued on as master's chief steward. Shortly afterwards, we met and married, and before long were anticipating the birth of our very first child. You were born on a

windy, rainy, cold night," mama said, softly rubbing
my hair.

   I listened intently.

   "Your father was afraid that he was about to lose
both of us during your birth, Ayala. It had proven to
be a very difficult delivery. Your tiny feet were coming first. He traveled in the cold, sleet and rain to get
to a woman who could help deliver you safely,"
mama said. "During those stormy-conditions, it
wasn't advisable for anyone to be outside. Yet, your
father's fear drove him. So, he set out to bring the
midwife home to help get the baby out. While trav-
eling, the wagon's wheel became lodged in the thick
mud caused by all of the rain. Your father fought the
sleet and cold trying to free it. The midwife reported
how he stayed in those inclement conditions for
hours fighting with the wheel until it finally bounced
loose. The midwife said she tried offering your father shelter under the ram-skin-blanket he had provided her with but he refused,—demanding she stay
covered under the wagon's thick canopy for her own
protection. Your father finally made it home, and
with the mid-wife's assistance, the most beautiful
baby girl in the world was born," mama gushed. "We
named you, Ayala."

   Sadness crept into mama's eyes as she told the
rest of the story.

   "As a result of the bitter cold and rain, your father
became quite ill with a deep cough, and fever. No
matter how hard we tried, he never seemed to get
any better but only grew worse. Each day, Ayala, he
would ask me to hold you up so that he could see his

beautiful baby girl. Those were the few times he would manage to smile. The illness left him bedridden for days. Unfortunately, when you were only one month old, your father died. Master whispered some special words to your father before he slipped away. He promised him he would always take care of you and me," mama said hugging me gently.

That story—while only shared a few times, and never in its entirety until now—always left me with a lingering sense of sadness. I often wondered what life would have been like had my father lived.

Either way, I was glad to be here, on the compound.

# Chapter Eight

As months passed along, conditions around the compound grew worse. Food was so limited we worked day and night to salvage the few crops that yielded any vegetables and fruit at the time. Master's health also continued to decline.

"Well, it's time for me to change his bed covering," I heard mistress say as she wiped the tiredness from her eyes.

"If you would like, I'll take care of it today," mama said. "You have done enough work for one day."

"No," mistress refused. "I have not seen him in a while. Besides, why should you be exposed to the stench inside that room? I will get it done."

I watched as mistress entered their bedchambers. Leaving the door open wide, I could easily listen in on their limited conversation. It was the first time they had spoken to each other in quite some time.

"How are you feeling?" mistress finally asked.

Even though it was more of a mumble, I somehow deciphered his words.

"Not well."

There was an awkward silence between the two when suddenly mistress cried out in anguish, "Are you praying and asking God what we should do, or are you just lying there awaiting death?"

"No, and yes," he quickly, replied.

I could tell the response was not the one mistress neither expected nor wanted to hear. Composing herself somewhat, she forged on.

"Why, not?" mistress asked, removing the blood-stained sheets. "Why aren't you praying—that is the least you could do?"

"He's not hearing me anymore. He won't listen," master stated, sourly.

Dropping the soiled linen, mistress looked over at him. "I need your help. I need you! Please fight for me... fight for us," mistress cried out.

His silence and aloofness proved to be more than she could bear.

"Don't you care anymore?" mistress asked in desperation.

Still... no response.

Eyes narrowed, she glared at him. "So, you are trying to hold on to your precious integrity, is that it?" Her entire body trembled as she spoke.

Silence........

"I see." Just then, it seemed everything inside of her exploded—the ire bursting forth like millions of poisonous arrows. "Then why... why....why don't you curse God and die?" mistress yelled, falling to her knees.

I gasped as soon as the incriminating words came pouring out from her lips. Nothing could have ever prepared me for the blistering statement that burned like hot- spewing lava. Catching myself so as not to tumble down from my secret spot, I forced back the tears. Even I knew how extremely wrong and hurtful words like that were.

It was master who had taught me to revere the God of Abraham, Isaac, and Jacob...as *The One* and only living God. He had often spoken of God's miraculous acts and of all His wonderous ways to me. When faced with insurmountable odds, it was master who would often ask me the question .... "Is there anything too hard for God?" He helped me understand like never before....that there was absolutely no problem God could not solve. He was *"The Master"* of the Universe whom I now served. I believed in *The One* who made heaven and earth—the God who spoke the world into existence by the breath of His Words and the moving of His Spirit.

All of that was what I had been taught by the man who was now sitting here so justifiably offended right now.

Is this the God mistress wanted master to curse? It could not be! I was not so sure mistress had not committed some type of crime...the kind of heinous act even punishable by stoning. If anyone else had heard her say those words, she would face persecution beyond anything she could have imagined.

How could I ever look at mistress the same way again? Who was this mean, harsh woman and where had the soft spoken princess I had grown to love, gone?

"Noooooo...this was not how mistress and master talked to each other," I thought.

Right then, a depressive force overshadowed me. It felt like a cloak draped in despair.

Not only was I going to have to deal with the grim manner in which they now spoke to each other, I also had to wrestle with the blasphemous statement mistress had just uttered.

*"Curse God and die...."* I played those words over and over as I braced myself for master's reply.

While the quietness filtered its way throughout the air, I held my breath until he finally spoke. His voice weakened by the illness, now suddenly sounded stronger than ever.

*"You speak as one of the foolish women. What do you expect... that we should receive only good from God, and not evil?"*

I waited for the dust to settle. I knew being called *foolish* was a level of dishonor mistress had never experienced before. By the look on her face, I understood how hard the words must have stung. It was the instant gasp, as she inhaled, and the sudden paleness that snatched the color from her face—that told me so. Her pallor resembled that of a corpse.

The death blow from the word *foolish* was what I knew she deserved.

Mistress never said a word after that damaging conversation. I watched as she calmly—perhaps too calmly—walk out the door and never look back.

Later that night, I waited for the light tap on our door as mistress had done ever since the darkness descended.

This time the knock on the door never came.

When mistress failed to show up at our bungalow, I tried to conceal my nervousness. It made matters worse the moment I noticed mama pacing back and forth. As the hour grew late, I watched mama wrap herself in her cloak and set out to find mistress.

I allowed a few minutes to go by before I grabbed my coat and tore out the door after her. Following close behind, yet avoiding being seen.... I spotted mistress at the edge of the compound's porch curled in a ball, shivering violently in the cold-damp, night air.

With only a thin gown protecting mistress from the bitter wind, it appeared she had allowed the chill to ravage her frail body. No one would have ever been able to withstand the cold temperatures, not even for a short period of time, especially dressed the way she was. I did not know how long mistress had been exposed to the elements, but based on her body's response, she should have gone inside a long time ago.

"Oh, no!" I heard mama scream. Taking off her cloak and wrapping mistress inside, mama held her tightly, allowing the warmth of her own body to generate the much-needed heat.

"Please, come into the house. Do not do this to yourself!" mama cried out. "Please!" mama pleaded.

"Let me die," mistress wept, her voice hoarse and cracked.

"How can I live and face the consequences of what I have done? How can I live considering all I have said to him? It is too much to bear. Death would be a welcomed comforter for me now," mistress said, coughing violently.

Mistress finally gave in to the coldness and despair, collapsing into mama's arms.

At that point, I ran with full-force towards the two desperate women. I gave no thought at all about being discovered. In a matter of seconds, I reached mama to help gather mistress up and take her inside.

We struggled at first to carry her, but the adrenalin soon rushed in. Before long, we were quickly carrying the dead-weight inside the house.

"Hurry Ayala, let's get her beside the fire," mama said, more frantic than I had ever seen her before.

"Get the blankets on the shelf over there....the extra thick ones. *Move*!"

Even though she spoke harshly, I knew mama wasn't angry with me for following along. I began pulling out the colorful quilts one by one. I raced back, quickly helping to warm mistress.

"Good. Now pour the hot water over those spices in the cup on the counter. Ayala, we must warm her up as fast as we can," mama said.

"Open your eyes," mama said, repeatedly tapping mistress' face. She rubbed her arms vigorously in an up and down fashion.

"Come on, that's it.... wake up," mama said.

"Oh-h-h, n-o-o-o," I heard mistress moan as her circulation began to improve.

Forcing the steamy brew down her throat, the deadly pallor covering mistress' face slowly waned as a pinch of color began to ease its way onto her cheeks.

"You should have let me die," were the first coherent words she spoke.

Mistress suddenly turned away from me and faced the wall. "I do not want the child to see me this way," she moaned.

At that moment, it was as if all the adrenalin that remained, found its way into my heart.

I wanted to scream, "It's too late mistress!   I have seen, and I have heard everything!"

# Chapter Nine

After the incident with mistress, I guess we paid little attention to anything else going on around the compound. Reminiscent of my father's misfortune resulting in his subsequent demise, mama and I devoted most of our time ensuring mistress did not succumb to a similar untimely death. It was only when I passed master's door that the importance of the day's events came as a reminder that something special was about to take place.

I turned my attention to the winding path leading up to the gate of the compound. There had been talk that special guests would soon arrive. I heard the two herdsmen who hung around speaking about the important men's arrival any day now.

"These are some of the wealthiest, wisest and most God-fearing men in the region," they whispered to each other. "Master's good friends are finally coming to see about him," the herdsmen said.

I had already made up my mind I was going to be there the moment the distinguished gentlemen showed up.

Even in his deteriorating condition, master had dressed to meet his special company. No longer dressed in the ragged outer apparel I had grown accustomed to, master now wore a neatly, loose fitting tunic. The garment still did little to cover the hideous sores that appeared all over his head, mouth and hands, but it was better than the blood-stained cloak.

As master crept slowly outside and away from his room—readying himself to meet his guest, I realized just how thin he had become. He was so emaciated and weakened, I worried an unexpected wind gust would easily carry him away.

The compound became eerily quiet at master's unexpected presence. As critical as his condition had become, putting forth the effort to greet these guests placed everything in perspective.

All eyes were now transfixed on the road leading to the main gate.

Finally, the much-anticipated visitors emerged.

Master set out to meet them, struggling—limping along, his body frail and feeble.

"Thank God the compound was ready for master's guests," I thought. Mama and I had prepared the quarters days ago.

I watched as four men slowly approached each other, easing themselves upon the cushioned mats onto the ground just inside the compound. Neither of the gentlemen spoke, including master while they all sat and stared.

As stunned as I was by master's, haggard, and wasted appearance, I knew each of these men had to be equally astounded. I watched and waited for hours to hear what they had to say to him, or to at least explain their presence. As time passed along, not a single word was exchanged between the four men. I thought it would be possible for me to outlast their silence, but mama summoned me to assist with the chores.

I hurried as fast as I could to feed the animals I had been assigned. The few we had left never seemed to want to cooperate when I was in a hurry.

Finally, finishing my errands, I raced back to the secret spot only to find the strange men once again sitting, staring at each other in amazement.

Eventually, I gave up for the day and went to find mama.

The next morning, I skipped breakfast and returned to hear if anything, master's guests had to say. For seven days I went back, time and time again, only to be confronted with the peculiar silence between the eccentric group. Each man's quietness seemed odd to me and was becoming somewhat distracting. I was beginning to wish they had never come.

***

The silence eventually drove me away.

I focused my attention back onto mistress and her spiraling emotional state.

As the menacing darkness continued, she no longer met mama outside of our bedchambers to discuss the day's affair. Instead, mama saw mistress to bed before we turned in for the night. She had even granted me permission to assist her with this new bedtime ritual. Mama's inclusion offered me a strange sense of freedom, eliminating the need to hide.

One night, as we all gathered in mistress' small sleeping quarters, I felt brave enough to bring up the matter of master and his friends.

"Our master sits with three men each day," I said, brushing the stubborn curl from out of mistress' hair.

"These are renowned men, *YaYa*, filled with Godly wisdom," mistress stated, weakly.

"Well, they have yet to offer my lord any help," I said. "Why did they come if they were just going to sit there and not communicate a word? Are they not able to extend at least a compassionate ear to him?"

"The men will speak. Give them time," mistress said softly.

# Chapter Ten

On the following day, as if they had heard mistress' prediction, it was master who finally opened up and initiated the dialogue.

Yet, as soon as master spoke, I soon wished he hadn't. A sudden, indescribable sense of sadness overwhelmed me. I listened to the man I most admired—grimly curse the day he was born. I shuddered as the harsh, icy words stung. He had told his three friends, he wished he had died at birth.

"*May the day of my birth perish, and the night that said, 'A boy is conceived!'*" I heard him cry out to them.

The tears flooded my eyes. I did all I could to fight them back, but I knew at this point, I had reached one of my lowest moments since the darkness fell upon us. As I listened on, the uncontrollable tears began to fall.

"*That day—may it turn to darkness; may God above not care about it; may no light shine on it. Let darkness and the shadow of death stain it...."Why did I not perish at birth, and die as I came from the womb? Why were there knees to receive me and breasts that I might be nursed? For now I would be lying down in peace; I would be asleep and at rest.*"

Hearing him long for death that way was beyond difficult—as though he and the detestable foe had become the best of friends. I prayed master would stop talking...but he simply would not.

*"....Why was I not hidden away in the ground like a stillborn child, like an infant who never saw the light of day? There the wicked cease from trouble, and there the weary are at rest."* he cried out. *"Captives also enjoy their ease; they no longer hear the slave driver's shout. The small and the great are there, and the slaves are freed from their owners."*

"Please, stop it! Just stop it!" I wanted to yell out to him. "How dare you chastise your wife for speaking so foolishly? What about yourself? Don't you hear what nonsense you speak right now?"

Then suddenly, I noticed one of the gentlemen preparing himself to speak. I listened attentively—anticipating what the one who called himself lord Eliphaz had to say. Perhaps he could talk some sense into master and help him understand how unwise it was to speak in such a fatalistic manner.

I felt an immediate sense of relief as the great man of wisdom began his oration. Sitting erect with his legs crisscrossed underneath him, he started out accurately describing the man I revered.

*"Think how you have instructed many,"* he started, slowly. *You have strengthened feeble hands. Your words have supported those who stumbled; you have strengthened faltering knees,"* he continued. *"Now trouble comes to you, and you are discouraged; it strikes you, and you are dismayed. Consider now: Who, being innocent, has ever perished? Where were the upright ever destroyed? As I have observed, those who plow evil and those who sow trouble reap it."*

Just like that, all my hopes of comfort were dashed! "Oh, my goodness," I thought, "What nonsense was this wise man spouting? Was he really suggesting that master had done something dreadfully wrong and was being punished for it?"

I listened on hoping that was not the case.

*"Call if you will, but who will answer you? To which of the holy ones will you turn? Resentment kills a fool, and envy slays the simple." ..."Blessed is the one whom God corrects; so do not despise the discipline of the Almighty."*

"Enough!" I wanted to scream at him. My hands trembled as I reached up and pressed hard on my throbbing temples. I tried to minimize the pain taking place in my head right then. "Can't you see what you are doing to him?" I wanted to yell. "You are causing him more harm than good!"

Now, I wished these three men had never come. In fact, I wished none of this was happening. My heart raced as I awaited master's response.

His next words confirmed my worst fears.

*"If only my anguish could be weighed and all my misery be placed on the scales,"* master cried aloud. *"It would surely outweigh the sand of the seas....."*

"Was this wise man sent here to finish killing master?" I wondered. The only visitor master finally had—had come with loathsome news and wrong advice.

I listened as master moaned and bewailed the counsel offered.

*"The arrows of the Almighty are in me, my spirit drinks in their poison; God's terrors are marshaled*

*against me......Oh, that I might have my request, that*
*God would grant what I hope for, that God would be*
*willing to crush me, to let loose his hand and cut off my*
*life! ... Even my own brethren have dealt deceitfully as*
*a brook...as the stream of brooks they pass away."*

I winced at the pain-laden words spoken by a
man filled with trouble and grief.

Everything around master was crumbling and it
was obvious he was nearing the end of his rope.

His own family had longed stopped coming to
visit him and rarely sent messages inquiring of his
well-being.  The pain settled in further as master's
brothers and sisters who benefited from the pleas-
ures of his wealth seemed to have forgotten him.

To further complicate matters, I wanted to believe that master had not noticed how badly things
were slowly falling apart around the compound.
Housed in his room day and night, I thought for sure
knowledge of our struggles had somehow escaped
him. Yet, when I heard him speak today, I knew it
wasn't so.

*"When I lie down I think, 'How long before I get*
*up?' The night drags on, and I toss and turn until*
*dawn."*

Master was aware of the compound's slow dete-
rioration.  His inability to sleep afforded him ample
opportunity to hear conversations taking place during the stillness of the night.

I listened on as master cried out in anguish....
*"When I think my bed will comfort me and my couch*
*will ease my complaint, even then you frighten me*

*with dreams and terrify me with visions, so that I pre-fer strangling and death, rather than this body of mine..... If I have sinned, what have I done to you, you who see everything we do? Why have you made me your target? Have I become a burden to you? Why do you not pardon my offenses and forgive my sins? For I will soon lie down in the dust; you will search for me, but I will be no more."*

"No-o-o-o! Master, please stop," I thought, shaking my head.

What had he done so horribly wrong that he did not believe God would forgive him? While I understood there is no one perfect except God, master came closer than any man I knew to being blameless. In fact, he shunned those who practiced evil or even the appearance of it.

I braced myself when I noticed the other man of wisdom preparing himself to speak. I would have hoped he'd chosen a better choice of words than the one before, but I wasn't so sure any more. I listened carefully as lord Bildad now faced master. He was a lot more animated in his delivery than his previous counter-part.

*"How long will you say such things? Your words are a blustering wind. Does God pervert justice? Does the Almighty pervert what is right?"* lord Bildad began his dialogue. *"When your children sinned against him, he gave them over to the penalty of their sin.... but if you will seek God earnestly and plead with the Almighty, if you are pure and upright, even now he will rouse himself on your behalf and restore you to your prosperous state."*

Okay, I had had enough! Who was this so-called man of wisdom who would dare suggest master was hiding wrongdoings and that his sons had paid the ultimate punishment for committing theirs.

A fist full of anger punched me hard in my gut.

I cannot stand to listen to another second of these unscrupulous words! I turned my back to storm off, but the sound of master's voice stopped me in my tracks.

*"Indeed, I know that this is true,"* he agreed. *"Yet, how can mere mortals prove their innocence before God? His wisdom is profound, his power is vast. Who has resisted him and come out unscathed? He moves mountains without their knowing it and overturns them in his anger. He shakes the earth from its place and makes its pillars tremble. He speaks to the sun and it does not shine; he seals off the light of the stars. He alone stretches out the heavens and treads on the waves of the sea."* master touted. *"Even if I summoned him and he responded, I do not believe he would give me a hearing. He would crush me with a storm and multiply my wounds for no reason. He would not let me catch my breath but would overwhelm me with misery."*

I could hardly believe what I was hearing.

I sat on the ground and cradled my head. I really didn't care if anyone saw me at that point. Was this master? Was this the man who taught me all about Israel's God, now agreeing with these wretched counselors?

The only good tiding I heard thus far was the manner in which master described the God of our Fathers.

I found God to be exactly the way master taught me. Every day and night I prayed to that same God who I learned was able to do anything but fail. He was the miracle working God who destroyed armies mightier than the ones any man could fashion together. He was the God who illuminated the sky by day and lit up the firmament by night. This was the Holy One of Israel whom I served. He was *The One* who always provided me with the comforts of a loving home and a caring mother.

He alone was my God.

"If they would all just keep silent and pray, perhaps God would turn things around for master," I thought.

It was all wishful thinking. The next few words dampened my spirits even more.

*"It should have been as though I had not been; I should have been carried from the womb to the grave. Are not my days few? Cease then and let me alone,"* master said. *"That I may take comfort a little before I go whence I shall not return, even to the land of darkness and the shadow of death..."*

Do good; live righteously, and God will bless you. That was what master always told me. It was how he lived his life, and I knew firsthand just how blessed master had become as a result. Now, it was strange to hear him speak of his own life as one of folly.

As for these two men, how dare they accuse him of having committed a crime so severe that the omniscient God needed to punish him?

I held my breath as the third man gathered himself to speak. It was not long before I had every reason in the world to wish these men had never come. Lord Zophar seemed menacing and was far worse than the other two.

*"Are all these words to go unanswered? Is this talker to be vindicated? Will your idle talk reduce others to silence?"* I heard lord Zophar say. *"Will no one rebuke you when you mock? You say to God, 'My beliefs are flawless and I am pure in your sight.' Oh, how I wish that God would speak, that he would open his lips against you and disclose to you the secrets of wisdom, for true wisdom has two sides. Know this: God has even forgotten some of your sin…… Surely he recognizes deceivers; and when he sees evil, does he not take note?"*

I became so furious at his misguided words, I slammed my eyes close tightly. For a moment, I thought about risking it all. Behind each phrase I wanted to jump up from the hiding place, point my finger in each of their faces and dare them to ever speak to master like that again.

"You are not men of wisdom….no sirs, you are not! Your words are void of understanding and as hollow as an empty well," I wanted to yell at them.

When a calmer voice prevailed, I pondered over a much more sensible solution. What if I were to tell mistress what was happening with the invited guests in her home? Perhaps she could talk some sense into this unconventional group. Before giving the thought further stock, I eventually set it aside. How was I ever going to let it be known what harm these men were doing without exposing my well-guarded secret? I had been told multiple times not to linger long, listening in on master's conversations—or as they would like to say, *"grown-folk affairs"*.

Besides, with the state of mind mistress was in, she might have easily agreed with these three gentlemen.

I left my secret place for the day and decided to find mama.

# Chapter Eleven

The next day and the weeks to follow, from my secret place I listened in on these miserable counselors.

My only hope was that master would soon snap out of this ill-advised fog. I knew him well. He would eventually come to his senses. It was his illness talking—not the loving, kind man that helped everybody.

I positioned myself so that I could take a better look into my master's eyes. I wanted to peer into the soul of the man that had given me hope in God.

I listened as he spoke.....

*"My eyes have seen all this, my ears have heard and understood it. What you know, I also know; I am not inferior to you. But I desire to speak to the Almighty and to argue my case with God. You, however, smear me with lies; you are worthless physicians, all of you! If only you would be altogether silent! For you, that would be wisdom."*

"Yes..... At last! I wanted to cry out. That's it! Let them have it! After all, you have been the one dealing with these unfortunate calamities—not them! How could men of such upright character be so brutal? It is comforting words that are needed right now, not this nonsense," I screamed silently.

Drawing the cool air in, I longed for my anxious-ness to settle.  I exhaled deeply, paying close atten-tion to what master said next.

*"Keep silent and let me speak; then let come to me what may. Why do I put myself in jeopardy and take my life in my hands?  Though he slay me, yet will I trust in him; I will surely defend my ways to His face....."* He continued, *"Men, born of woman, are of few days and full of trouble. They spring up like flowers and wither away; like fleeting shadows, they do not endure.... "If only you would hide me in the grave and conceal me till your anger has passed! If only you would set me a time and then remember me!  If someone dies, will they live again? All the days of my appointed time I will wait til my change come."*

I had had enough.  I ran as fast as I could to my sleeping quarters and prepared for bed.  Mama was surprised to see me there when she entered the room.

"Are you not feeling well?" she asked.  "You have taken to bed quite early, are you okay?"

"I'm fine.  Just a little tired," I said.

I kissed mama good night in hopes of alleviating her fears.  I was not one bit surprised, however, when she placed her hand on my forehead to check my body temperature.

"Okay.  Have a good night's rest," mama said, fi-nally letting the reason for my early bedtime, tempo-rarily go by.

I knew I had more work to do convincing her that all was well.

I did not know how mama did it, but I was sure she had mastered the art of discernment. In fact, I came to the conclusion that the gift was even deeper than that.

I was sure of it.

Mama was a mind-reader.

I turned over, wrapping my body entirely under the protective covering of the heavy quilt. I needed to slow the racing thoughts zipping through my head for the moment—knowing full well mama would soon be asking me about them.

She always did.

Even though I sought it, sleep never came. Like the nights before, I tossed and turned unable to find comfort in rest's soothing arms. Nothing bothered me more than hearing master speak of his great desire to die.

"Master looked as if death would soon carry him away, and his pleas only served to expedite its arrival," I thought. So, I wished he would stop using words like that.

Finally, after much wrestling, I found myself tumbling down the dark corridors of a troubled night's sleep. It was master's voice I heard echoing in the distance as I yielded to my heavy eyelids. The words of master bounced off the walls of my dream.... *"Though He slay me....yet will I trust in Him."*

The next morning, hesitant to unwrap myself from the warmth of the cozy blankets, the bright sun reminded me it was time to get moving. Creeping out of bed, I inched towards the basin. The cool water on my face quickly revived me. Slipping into my decorative tunic I reached for my sandals and fastened them on.   I wanted to make sure my chores were complete and that I ate every bite of the meal I knew mama had prepared.  Hopefully, acting as normal as possible would prolong the suspicion I knew was already lurking around in that mind of hers.

Engaging in conversation regarding my plans for the day, I sat calmly in the dining area, forcing down all of my breakfast.  I finally eased out of the door.

My errands took longer than I had anticipated. Many of my chores had gone unattended, and it was taking me more time to complete them.   I hated to do so, but I had to leave a few unfinished.  It was getting close to lunch and I had not yet visited my secret place.

Soon, I was off like a flash to hear the day's exchange between the clandestine men who I was convinced should never have come and would never understand master's plight.

When I arrived and settled in the corner of the hidden cavern right above them, I found the men already engrossed in vigorous discussion.   Lord Eliphaz seemed even more intense than I recalled on yesterday.  I listened as he spoke.....

*"Would a wise person answer with empty notions or fill their belly with the hot east wind?"* he said, in a very loud voice.  *"Would they argue with useless words, with speeches that have no value....but you even undermine piety and hinder devotion to God. Your sin prompts your mouth; you adopt the tongue of the crafty. Your own mouth condemns you, not mine; your own lips testify against you.  Are you the first man*

*ever born? Were you brought forth before the hills? Do you listen in on God's council? Do you have a monopoly on wisdom? What do you know that we do not know? What insights do you have that we do not have?"*

It was obvious I had missed a portion of this heated conversation prior to my arrival. I could tell by the look on master's face he was upset.

All of the men were.

In fact, they each seemed angry—even hostile.

*"If God places no trust in his holy ones, if even the heavens are not pure in his eyes, how much less mortals, who are vile and corrupt, who drink up evil like water! Listen to me and I will explain to you; let me tell you what I have seen,"* lord Eliphaz said, now clearly agitated. *"Even what the wise have declared, hiding nothing received from their ancestors (to whom alone the land was given when no foreigners moved among them): All his days the wicked man suffers torment, the ruthless man through all the years stored up for him.........Distress and anguish fill him with terror; troubles overwhelm him, like a king poised to attack, because he shakes his fist at God and vaunts himself against the Almighty defiantly charging against him with a thick, strong shield.... He will no longer be rich and his wealth will not endure, nor will his possessions spread over the land. He will not escape the darkness;... and the breath of God's mouth will carry him away."*

"Okay," I thought. "It was time for me to apply my own deductive reasoning to this critical situation since it was obvious these men were not going to do so. I tossed around a few questions I felt deserved sensible deliberation. First, I wanted to know, what purpose did it serve grand men who exuded great wisdom to completely ignore the apparent good residing within this honorable man? They knew master well and all he had done for others. Did they believe God was going to ignore those acts of kindness also? Secondly, they seemed to be convinced that as long as master did what was right, God would be willing to bless him. That appeared to be the consensus of the three. The problem was that when master did something wrong—it negated all the good he had done in the past—and therefore, God was punishing him and taking everything away.

That made no sense!

Was this the point they wanted conveyed to her master?

The answer tapped her on the shoulder.

Indeed it was… however wrong it may be.

These men believed master had committed a crime so egregious; God was punishing him for it despite all the good locked inside of him. Believing they were qualified to proclaim such a fact, they hurled insult after insult toward master, willingly and without remorse. Their ancestral lineage gave them the right to do so. After all, *"It was their fathers who'd passed generations of wisdom and knowledge along to them,"* I had heard each of them boast.

The picture was becoming clearer now.

These were men who felt they had the legal authority to speak with conviction and assurance about master and God. They came to the conclusion

God only rewarded men for the good that they did, and punished them for the evil. It was also their belief that master was immoral and in desperate need of repenting.

It was master's voice that broke my concentration.

*"I have heard many things like these,"* he said. *"You are miserable comforters, all of you! Will your long-winded speeches never end?...I also could speak like you, if you were in my place; I could make fine speeches against you and shake my head at you... But my mouth would encourage you; comfort from my lips would bring you relief."*

Tears flooded my eyes, again. Oh, how I wished these frail men would cease hurting master. If only they knew how much further encouraging words would benefit him right now. Master's heart was bleeding, and they were doing nothing to stop it.

It was getting close to lunch time, and I was already growing tired of listening to master's travail.

*"Surely, God, you have worn me out; you have devastated my entire household,"* he cried out. *"You have shriveled me up—and it has become a witness; my gauntness rises up and testifies against me. God assails me and tears me in his anger and gnashes his teeth at me; my opponent fastens on me his piercing eyes. People open their mouths to jeer at me; they strike my cheek in scorn and unite together against me. God has turned me over to the ungodly and thrown me into the clutches of the wicked. All was well with me, but he shattered me; he seized me by the neck and crushed me. He has made me his target"*

If it were possible for me to feel any worse than I already did, fate had somehow stepped in to increase my pain. Was master speaking this harshly about God now? I have never known him to talk unkindly to anyone,—let alone God.

I listened as master began to question God, as the wise men flung cruel, heart-wrenching words at him.

*"When will you end these speeches? Be sensible, and then we can talk."* lord Bildad yelled at master. *"....The lamp of a wicked man is snuffed out; the flame of his fire stops burning... The vigor of his step is weakened; his own schemes throw him down. Calamity is hungry for him; disaster is ready for him when he falls. It eats away parts of his skin; death's firstborn devours his limbs...The memory of him perishes from the earth; he has no name in the land.... He has no offspring or descendants among his people, no survivor where once he lived....People of the west are appalled at his fate; those of the east are seized with horror. Surely such is the dwelling of an evil man; such is the place of one who does not know God."*

I gasped at the stinging words. No one in a million years would ever believe what this man just said. The conversation had gone to another whole level of disrespect. Had he just suggested master's iniquity was so great he did not know God?

I was numb.

I awaited master's response....

*"If it is true that I have gone astray, my error remains my concern alone. If indeed you would exalt yourselves above me and use my humiliation against me, then know that God has wronged me and drawn*

*his net around me.  Though I cry, 'Violence!' I get no response; though I call for help, there is no justice... He has stripped me of my honor and removed the crown from my head.  He tears me down on every side till I am gone; he uproots my hope like a tree.  His anger burns against me; he counts me among his enemies."*

I could not stand another minute of these depressing arguments.

What master said about God was more than I could bear.  I turned to leave when I caught the tail end of these chilling words......

*"He has alienated my family from me; my acquaintances are completely estranged from me.  My relatives have gone away; my closest friends have forgotten me."*

I knew master was not only speaking of his brothers, but in my heart I understood he was also speaking about me and mama.

It was true.

We had not spoken to or seen master in months.  He had every right to believe he had been left alone and deserted.  The piercing words felt like pain from the initial thrust of a hunter's knife penetrating exposed skin.  It was excruciating and his account regarding each of us forsaking him—drove the blade in deeper.

*"My guests and my female servants count me a foreigner; they look on me as on a stranger.  I summon my servant, but he does not answer, though I beg him with my own mouth.  My breath is offensive to my wife; I am loathsome to my own family.  Even the little boys*

*scorn me; when I appear, they ridicule me. All my in-*
*timate friends detest me; those I love have turned*
*against me. I am nothing but skin and bones; I have*
*escaped only by the skin of my teeth. Have pity on me,*
*my friends, have pity, for the hand of God has struck*
*me? Why do you pursue me as God does? Will you*
*never get enough of my flesh?"*

I turned and raced to the shed where the few animals were kept, and fell into a corner piled with
straw. I cannot remember ever crying so hard.

I did not go back to my secret place for the rest of
the day. Those words chased me away, and my coun-
tenance could not be lifted no matter how hard I
tried.

Master felt abandoned and isolated. He was pen-
niless and his body infested with weeping sores
causing him to be shunned by anyone who dared encounter him. I saw how the servants treated him
now, and I hated them for that.

I felt helpless. I had no reasonable solutions.

Later, that night and void of an appetite, I finally
drifted off to sleep. My rest was disturbed as I was
being chased by the villain who starred in my tor-
turous dreams. Catching up to me, a heavy-dark
presence of evil affixed a vice-like grip around my
neck and squeezed. I awakened, violently gasping
for air.

For the next few days, I stayed away from my secret hide-out. To limit the unnecessary worry, and
to free my mind from the tormenting dreams, I buried myself into the many chores needing to be ac-
complished around the compound.

"I really appreciate you taking on these additional duties, Ayala," mama said.

I never looked up at her when she spoke. I was afraid she would see the story my eyes now told.

Putting space between me and the dismal conversation was the welcomed break I needed. After a few days, however, my curiosity got the best of me and I longed to know what the men were saying to master. Most of all, I wanted to check in to see how well he was fairing, considering the condition he was in the last time I saw him.

I could not help but wonder if anyone else understood the impact the meeting these so-called men were having on all of us. The only reason the few of us remained on the compound was because master was barely clinging to life. Did anybody know how close we were to losing him...how close we were to leaving and losing everything?

I needed to check on him today.

As I eased out of bed before mama aroused, I hurried to finish my chores. Perhaps the men's troubling conversations had ended on a better note this time.

I didn't want to miss any more of it.

# Chapter Twelve

Once I began the routine of visiting my secret place again, I could not resist the temptation of going back each day. Every free moment, I listened to these alleged great men of wisdom as they berated my noble master.

*"God does not accuse a holy man, yet God accuses you, because you are very evil,"* lord Eliphaz, said.

The level of disrespect coming from these men was unfathomable. I knew it was the only reason my nightmares increased. It was lord Eliphaz's face I frequently saw chasing mama in the darkness in several of them.

My opinion of these unrepentant men had dwindled, and I never wanted them to return to our sacred compound again. I did not consider any of them wise, and now realized the depth of heartlessness that crouched in their empty souls.

*"You have done so many evil deeds,"* lord Eliphaz, continued. *"When you lent even a small loan, you forced your brothers to hand over their property. You even took their clothes, so that they were naked. You did not provide water for people who were weak. You did not provide food for hungry people. But you were a powerful man, who owned much land. You were a man whom people respected. You gave nothing to widows. You caused children to suffer. And those children had no fathers to protect them. This is why you*

*have so many troubles. This is why you are suddenly
afraid.  You are like a man who cannot see in the darkness. Then a flood drowns that man. But God is in the
highest heavens. His home is even higher than the
stars. But you say, 'God does not know about me. He
cannot see me because of the darkness. Thick clouds
surround God, so that he does not see us. He belongs in
heaven.....This is why I refuse to obey a wicked man's
advice. A good man is glad when evil men suffer." (Job
22: 4-19)*

"Ayala," I heard mama cry out.

I recognized the tone in her voice, and knew trouble was on the horizon.  I scurried away from my secret place.

"Yes, ma'am?"

"Where have you been?  I have been looking everywhere for you," mama said, scolding me.

I stood silently as I forced back my tears.  Once
they were tucked safely away, I spoke, hoping the
tremor in my voice went unnoticed.

"I wanted to make sure master and his friends
didn't need anything, so....."

"Do not ever go near that room again.  Do you understand?" mama interjected before I was able to finish my explanation.

"Yes, I understand."

"I know all about that secret hide-out of yours,
and I forbid you to go near it.  Do you hear me,
Ayala?"

"Yes, I hear you," I repeated.

"The mind-reader had done it again!" I thought. It was the rare edge in her voice, however, that made it clear I had no other choice but to obey.

During the long night in my room, I covered my head so the silent tears streaming down could not be seen. My body shook as I cried out silently in pain. My heart was breaking. It was right before mama had called out to me, that I heard master utter these words....

*"Even today my complaint is bitter; his hand is heavy in spite of my groaning. If only I knew where to find him; if only I could go to his dwelling! I would state my case before him and fill my mouth with arguments. I would find out what he would answer me, and consider what he would say to me. Would he vigorously oppose me? No, he would not press charges against me. There the upright can establish their innocence before him, and there I would be delivered forever from my judge. But if I go to the east, he is not there; if I go to the west, I do not find him. When he is at work in the north, I do not see him; when he turns to the south, I catch no glimpse of him. But he knows the way that I take; when he has tested me, I will come forth as gold. "But he stands alone, and who can oppose him? He does whatever he pleases. He carries out his decree against me, and many such plans he still has in store. That is why I am terrified before him; when I think of all this, I fear him. God has made my heart faint; the Almighty has terrified me. Yet I am not silenced by the darkness, by the thick darkness that covers my face."*

\*\*\*

After a few days passed, I was actually thankful mama made me stay away from the place I thought was my top secret. Apparently, it had not been much of a secret at all.

The perceptive-one—better known as mama, knew all about it.

However, a sudden sense of pride welled up in me. I was convinced she did not know about all of my secret places.

Finally, I had out-smarted her.

As time passed, I was getting used to not going to my secret hide-out. I had my fill of the comfortless words spoken there. Besides, those arguments spoken by the so-called wise men only served as a constant reminder of the grave trouble we were all in.

At this point, I understood the seriousness of the conditions of the compound better than anyone else. The moment the servants began to withdraw the level of respect this great man of statue deserved—I knew it was only a matter of time before it all crumbled around us. I heard them talking about him....never tending to him when he called. It infuriated me because I knew when he was well he took great care of the very ones who neglected him now. I realized they treated him poorly because they felt he was no better off than they were.

"So what if master had nothing left," I reasoned with myself. It was never his possessions that drew me to him anyway. It was his kind and caring heart that did.

I had done all I knew to do to help mistress and master, and so had mama. While we barely had enough to eat, I never complained.  Even though the chores were insurmountable, I tried my best to complete them all.  I understood there was no way for me to accomplish the tasks I had been assigned, but still, I tried.  Mama never chastised me anymore about not finishing them.

It all became hopeless when I overheard mama say we would soon be leaving as well.  Mistress was forcing her out.

"Take Ayala away from this dreadful life, filled with misery," I heard mistress say.

# Chapter Thirteen

"This was the only land I had known and loved," I thought. "Uz was home...a place where I blossomed—where I felt alive. It overflowed with great harvests year after year....livestock, produce, family and friends were all in abundance. It was an oasis of hope where I stood steadfast that all my wishes and dreams would one day come true. There was a noble man awaiting for me out there—someone very much like master. He would carry me away to another fine home and I would fill it with wonderful sons and daughters of my own. I refused to believe this was how the fate of people who had lived righteous lives would end. A place left with a hollowed shell of a home, filled with overgrown crops and empty stalls—no longer illuminating with cheerfulness and brightness, a dull-darkened film surrounding every inch of its walls.....

Was this our destiny?

Even the light in mistress' eyes dimmed further as she sat in her darkened room alone most of the day. It was now mama and me who carried the majority of the load around the compound. Only a handful of the faithful servants would occasionally drop in to lend a helping hand. The only other person who called on us was one more of the miserable comforters. His name was lord Elihu. He was younger than the rest—his voice strong and vibrant.

I could tell he was void of glad tidings too. Attending to my daily chores one day, I took the opportunity to glance into the room where they all sat. The looks on each of their faces confirmed that nothing had changed.

As the days passed, the yearning that had escaped me, returned. Again, I longed to know what master and now the great men of four, discussed. While my secret place beacon hard for me, it never overshadowed the obedience and respect I willingly gave mama.

"Ayala, come and sit with me," mama called out to me one day.

As I rested on the pillows beside her, I laid my head in mama's lap.

"We will soon be leaving the compound," she said, gently stroking the curls that filled my hair.

"My father's brother has agreed to let us come live with him for a while. I am sure you will like it there. He has a nice home with maidens your age that live there also. I know how much you love our master and mistress, but God has other plans for us now."

"What will happen to them?" I asked, fighting back the tears. "Mama, how will master and mistress live?"

"I don't know....but I do know God will take care of them too," mama said. "I am sure of that."

I hugged mama tightly, wanting so badly to tell her all that I hid deep inside. The secret places had taught me a lot. It had given me access to infor-mation I was convinced no one else had... "Not even you," I wanted to cry out to mama.

"They won't be okay if we leave," I held back tell-ing her.

Realizing it was too late to share any of that.... all during the night, I poured out everything I had hid-den in my heart to the one I knew would under-stand......God.

# Chapter Fourteen

Like old times, that night, the two friends sat on the steps in front of our living quarters. I watched and listened through the tiny hole.

"You're right, I must consider Ayala's well-being more than anyone else at this point," I heard mama say.

"You must take her away," mistress said. "The food is so limited I am afraid for her to lose any more weight than she already has."

"I understand," mama responded.

"In a few days, I am expecting them to seize control of the compound anyway. The taxes are too far behind I was told. One of the neighbors was kind enough to let me in on their plans. I wanted you to know so that you and '*YaYa* can move away as quickly as you can."

The words must have tapped the tender spots on each of their hearts as I watched the tears fall from their eyes. At that moment, I didn't even mind being called, '*YaYa*.

"I never wanted to leave you mistress. I'm afraid if I don't take this last opportunity, it may not end well for Ayala," mama said, silently weeping.

"Sh-h-h, please don't cry," mistress said.

This time, it was strange to witness mama fall into the consoling arms of mistress as she helped soothe the pain of leaving the compound now caused.

As I recall, that was the last night the two women ever met on our porch.

***

"Ayala," mistress called out to me. "Please take this tea to my lord and his friends."

I watched as mistress' thin hands trembled while handing me the serving dish.

"Yes, mistress," I said, reaching for the clay platter.

I refused to look directly into her eyes. I knew the sadness surrounding them was a result of us leaving soon.

I held on tightly to the clay platter. I quickly turned my head and left the room to find mama.

"Mistress has asked that I take this to my lord and his guests," I said.

I never wanted mama to think I would ever disobey her rules. Getting permission before going into them I knew was a necessity.

Mama nodded, as she packed our belongings.

"Hurry back Ayala, a storm is approaching," she yelled out to me as I rushed out the door.

"Yes, ma'am," I yelled back. It was difficult to hide my enthusiasm.

The excitement intensified as I drew near the room.

I could faintly hear their conversation again as I approached the room where the five men sat. Never acknowledging my presence, I quickly served each man, and eased my way out.

My secret place stared hard at me as I looked up slowly at it. Finally, yielding in to its hypnotic grasp, like a ghost in the night, I ran to my familiar spot and listened. It was lord Elihu now speaking. I had to strain to hear due to the rumbling of the thunder overhead and the howls of the gusting winds

*"This storm excites me,"* he said. *"My heart beats hard. I can feel the movements of my own heart. Listen! Listen to the noise (of the storm)! That noise is like God's own voice. From heaven, God sends the lightning. God causes the lightning to strike across the world. The sound called thunder is after the lightning. This is like the sound of God's voice. It is so powerful. God's voice surprises us. He does great things that we cannot explain. He tells the snow, 'Fall down to the ground!' And he says to the rain, 'Become a powerful storm!' God causes every man to stop work. So, they see the work of God. The animals hide. Or, they stay in their homes. Strong winds blow. And the weather becomes cold. God causes ice. The lakes freeze. God supplies water to the clouds. And he scatters lightning through the clouds. He directs the movement of clouds across the world. The clouds do whatever God orders. He might use the clouds to punish men (by a terrible storm). Or, he might provide rain because he loves the people on the earth.*

So engrossed by this young man's words, I failed to notice the black clouds hovering overhead like before. I had been away far too long and the unfamiliarity of his speech captivated me beyond measure. Ignoring everything around me, I listened on.

*"Now no one can look at the sun, bright as it is in the skies after the wind has swept them clean. Out of the north he comes in golden splendor; God comes in awesome majesty. The Almighty is beyond our reach and exalted in power; in his justice and great righteousness, he does not oppress. Therefore, people revere him, for does he not have regard for all the wise in heart?"* lord Elihu asked.

From out of nowhere, the gusty wind fastened me hard against the solid wall. I tried to force myself free from the wind's grasp, but I found its grip too strong. My screams, now muffled by the wind's screeching howls, were easily overpowered and could not be heard.

A violent blow—a strike—something happened that caused the bright light to appear—its illumination beyond description. I held on to nothing as I floated effortlessly into the whimsical arms of thin air. There was nothing in all of life's experiences to compare to the beauty and calming effect the light's presence had upon me. I knew I had never been to a place like this before and was glad I had come. Immediately, the fear that engulfed me moments ago vanished away. Not even the protection of mama's loving arms could suffice for where ever I found myself now. The indescribable love so deep and pure that swept softly over me pulled me further in. I felt I had no other choice but to follow the pathway to its origin. Floating there, it led me to a fountain of water that seemed familiar. Emitting grace, mercy, love and joy—I allowed each to take turns showering me with its fragrance.

I had decided I was never going to leave this place.

Lifted high above master and his guest, I heard the familiar sound of *The One* I had heard speak before. Even though the Voice had never spoken to me in that manner, it was still very much recognizable. Dressed in white—beyond any whiteness I had ever seen before, *The One* who spoke towered over master and said these unforgettable words...

*"Who is this that obscures my plans with words without knowledge? Brace yourself like a man; I will question you, and you shall answer me."*

His Voice.....was like the rushing of many waters, now began to drive unimaginable fear deep into my heart. "How did I ever deserve the privilege of being in His presence?" I thought. I cowered under the might of His magnetic Words......

*"Where were you when I laid the earth's foundation? Tell me, if you understand. Who marked off its dimensions? Surely you know! Who stretched a measuring line across it? On what were its footings set, or who laid its cornerstone—while the morning stars sang together and all the angels shouted for joy? Who shut up the sea behind doors when it burst forth from the womb, when I made the clouds its garment and wrapped it in thick darkness, when I fixed limits for it and set its doors and bars in place, I said, 'This far you may come and no farther; here is where your proud waves halt'? Have you ever given orders to the morning, or shown the dawn its place, that it might take the earth by the edges and shake the wicked out of it? ..... Have you journeyed to the springs of the sea or walked*

*in the recesses of the deep? Have the gates of death been shown to you? Have you seen the gates of the deepest darkness?...Tell me, if you know all this. What is the way to the abode of light? And where does darkness reside? .... Surely you know, for you were already born! You have lived so many years! Have you entered the storehouses of the snow or seen the storehouses of the hail, which I reserve for times of trouble, for days of war and battle? What is the way to the place where the lightning is dispersed, or the place where the east winds are scattered over the earth? Who cuts a channel for the torrents of rain, and a path for the thunderstorm, to water a land where no one lives, an uninhabited desert, to satisfy a desolate wasteland and make it sprout with grass? Does the rain have a father? Who fathers the drops of dew? From whose womb comes the ice? Who gives birth to the frost from the heavens when the waters become hard as stone, when the surface of the deep is frozen?... "Do you know when the mountain goats give birth? Do you watch when the doe bears her fawn? Do you count the months till they bear? Do you know the time they give birth? They crouch down and bring forth their young; their labor pains are ended."*

The look on master's face was enough to let me know—the awesome presence was now encompassing him as well. It was more than any man should be able to withstand. I understood why he fell down prostrate upon his face.

Despite master's humble submission, *The One* who carried the Voice of Many Waters grew relentless...*"Will the one who contends with the Almighty*

*correct him? Let him who accuses God answer him!"*
He said.

The frail and feeble voice of master attempted to answer.

*"I am unworthy—how can I reply to you? I put my hand over my mouth. I spoke once, but I have no an- swer— twice, but I will say no more."*

It was a thoroughly unfair exchange. The LORD quickly spoke back to him out of the great storm, and said, *"Brace yourself like a man; I will question you, and you shall answer me. Would you discredit my jus- tice? Would you condemn me to justify yourself? Do you have an arm like God's, and can your voice thun- der like his? Then adorn yourself with glory and splen- dor, and clothe yourself in honor and majesty......"*

Considering his only option, for the first time in quite a while, I listened to master speak. A man filled with truth and integrity, finally answered. It was the man I had missed—the one I had not heard nor seen in a very long time.....

*"I know that you can do all things; no purpose of yours can be thwarted. You asked, 'Who is this that obscures my plans without knowledge?' Surely I spoke of things I did not understand, things too wonderful for me to know. You said, 'Listen now, and I will speak; I will question you, and you shall answer me. My ears had heard of you but now my eyes have seen you. Therefore I despise myself and repent in dust and ashes."*

Apparently, the answer being sufficient enough, the Voice turned His attention to master's friends.

The commands towards them were worse.....

*"I am angry with you and your two friends, be-
cause you have not spoken the truth about me, as my
servant has,"* He said, to lord Eliphaz. *"So now take
seven bulls and seven rams and go and sacrifice a
burnt offering for yourselves. My servant will pray for
you, and I will accept his prayer and not deal with you
according to your folly. You have not spoken the truth
about me, as my servant has."*

Like a flash, *The One* whose Voice bellowed, was
no longer present. It was master who turned and ad-
dressed his friends now.

"Men, listen to me," he said. "At last, my God has
spoken and I have heard Him," he yelled out over the
wind. "I was rendered speechless when he offered
me His great questions...it was because I had no answers."

*"Did I decide when the morning would appear?"*
He asked me.

"How could I respond?" master asked. "Yet, He
would not yield. Again and again, God pounded me
with wisdom too great for me to answer. He spoke
of birds and animals, constellation and sea crea-
tures....and still, I had no answers," master con-
fessed. Finally, my brothers, the vastness of all I
understood Him to be surrounded me like a consum-
ing fire. With great revelation I was finally able to answer. I realized," I heard master scream out over the
wind... "I had uttered things that I did not understand. This omnipotent, sovereign God can do what
He chooses—how and whenever He decides to.
Good and bad things can indeed happen to good people. That does not mean when a man suffers he is no

longer good.  It simply means our God is sovereign, and we must still trust Him."

Master stood up taller than ever.  "As you can tell men of wisdom, I now repent in dust and ashes.  Listen to me…..  He is also angry with you because of your foolish counsel and I must pray for you."

Master lifted up both frail arms to heaven and cried…..

"I call upon the God of my Fathers….the God of Abraham, Isaac and Jacob….the Great God of the universe…..*The One* and only true and living God….," his voice boomed out loud.  "Be merciful unto each of us your servants as we bow in humble adoration before You.  We believe that You alone know all things and that You do all things well…. Our times… our earthly possessions and all that matter to us are in Your Hands.  Father, bless my friends, Eliphaz, Bildad, and Zophar.  Endow them with the kind of wisdom that only flows from You.  Let them be men of great counsel to all they encounter……Oh, my Father……"

His voice trailed off……

# Chapter Fifteen

"Ayala! Ayala! Please wake up," I heard mama cry out in the distance. "That's it, open your eyes, my precious baby."

"Oh-h-h," I moaned reaching for my head.

"Mother?" I asked, weakly.

"Yes, my beautiful one, I am here. Thank you, Father, oh thank you," I could hear the faint voice of mama cry.

I instantly remembered the bright light that held me captive seemingly for an eternity. Like a flash of thunder crawling across the midnight sky, something pushed me into a dark corridor, the light fading as I began opening my eyes. In the distance, I could visualize mama's face.

Eventually, things all around me began to become more focused. I tried repositioning myself, but the pain in my head instantly forced me to lie still on the soft, warm pillow.

"There, there. Not yet, you have to regain your strength first," mama whispered. "That's it open your eyes, Ayala."

I finally looked into mama's eyes and gently reached up to wipe the tears flowing from them.

Softly, taking my hands in hers, mama kissed each one of my small fingers and smiled. "I knew you were going to come back to me. God told me so."

Puzzled, I looked around and finally realized I was not resting in my own comfortable bed, but lying in mistress' bed-chamber, surrounded by the soft, pillows and sheets which now gently embraced me.

I held onto mama's hand, refusing to let it go.

***

Each time I drifted off and woke up again, I was glad to see mama had never left my bedside.

In fact, mama told me later that she had been there ever since the accident, and refused to leave.

After a few days, I was now fully awake and able to sit up in bed all by myself. Eventually the pain even left.

"Here take this," mama said, feeding me a spoon filled with the delicious stew.

"It will give you the strength you need to bounce back even faster," she smiled.

My thoughts were becoming clearer each day. The last thing I remembered was being pressed against the wall as I listened to master's wonderful prayer. Immediately when he had finished praying, in the far distance I could see his face, handsome and healthy as ever. He was once more tending to countless animals in the wide-open plain—giving orders to the many servants.

"What happened mother?" I asked. "How did I get here?"

"You were caught in the great storm, but mistress and I found you, and brought you here to safety. It was a large piece of the window's frame that caught the corner of your brow, Ayala. You have been asleep for two days."

"The storm...." I reached up and gently touched the bandage wrapped around my head.

"I know mama and it was wonderful. We don't have to leave master's house," I said, sitting up.

"He is well now and I know he will get everything back—and more!" I exclaimed. "You must go to him mama and see for yourself. He is well. I promise. Please!"

"Hush, Ayala. You took an awful fall when the wind knocked you down."

"No, mama, it's true," I interrupted. "I'm telling you I saw it. Please go and see for yourself."

"Is that our precious '*YaYa*?" mistress asked, entering the room. "Is she awake and talking? This has to be the most wonderful day of my life," she said, rushing to my bedside.

"She's telling some strange tale about master being well again," mama said, shaking her head.

"This is the day of miracles!" mistress exclaimed. "My '*YaYa* is fully back with us and so is my husband. I hadn't seen him since the storm, so I went in to see how he faired. I stood there in disbelief as I looked upon a man, clothed, and his skin healthier than I have seen it in a very long time. It is a miracle! I have hope again!

"I told you so," I screamed. "I saw him too, totally healthy and with all of his animals."

The two women looked at each other and smiled.

"When I walked into his room," mistress continued, "I was warmly greeted by his guests. Their faces shone brightly too—as if they all had been restored. My husband reached for me and told me to have hope again, that everything was going to be okay from now on. It was the first time in a very long time that he gave me reason to believe that we were going to make it out of this harrowing experience."

Mistress sat on the bed and softly wrapped her arms gently around me.

She looked at me—then at mama and said, "I realize God has given you back the one thing that is most important to you. Having Ayala awake and healthy is everything you wanted," she said softly, tears filling her eyes. My husband is finally gaining his strength and beginning to feel well again too. The great men of wisdom seem relieved. They are packing up and will be exiting the compound shortly. All of this is wonderful news for each one of you, but guess what," she said, gazing softly at me.

"I am restored too."

"I truly am."

# Chapter Sixteen

In no time, I was up and feeling like myself again. In fact, as the years passed, everything around the compound went back to normal.

Like all good mothers, mama kept a closer eye on me ever since the bump on the head. It was just mama exemplifying her caring and doting ways.

However, mama was beginning to realize that her daughter was no longer the little girl on the compound.

It seemed overnight I blossomed into this beautiful, young, very smart—woman.

***

Soon, I was racing around the compound trying to keep up with the smallest of mistress and master's growing family. This was my only assignment now, and it was indeed a prestigious one.

All the miracles I had seen in the bright light had finally come to pass. Everything I tried to tell them since my accident had come true.

After the great storm, master's family finally came to check on him. Once they arrived, they immediately began assisting in getting the compound back in order. The important men in the region also came and sat down with him. Shortly after their visit, cattle and all sorts of livestock began to show up. It was like the days of old as we all rejoiced and celebrated. However, it was when the prophet came to visit and told mistress what was needed to cure him completely, that rendered us all the happiest. After that, no trace of sickness could be found in master's body. He was handsome and healthy as ever.

Once master got back on his feet, the compound and all of his possessions grew larger than before. His assets had grown to such proportions, I had been given the responsibility of being "the maiden-in-charge". It was now my duty to ensure the household's assignments were given out and performed appropriately each day.

However, the best part of it all was that my relationship with God had blossomed beyond measure, and I was closer to Him more now than ever before.

I had come to realize no matter the circumstance—that God remained the same. His love, grace and mercy was available to everyone despite the difficulties that may arise.    Trials and afflictions do come upon the righteous, but God sees them safely through them all. God is a great Restorer and He will not withhold any good thing from His sons and daughters.

I understood more than anything else.... that He was not only master's God....but, was a wonderful God and Father to me as well.

I even gained true meaning behind mama's perceptive gift. It was her close relationship with God that always kept her a step ahead.

Mama was no mind-reader.

# Chapter Seventeen

I found myself in the wide-opened plain one day looking around—standing there taking it all in....absorbed by all the Lord had given us.

I breathed in a sigh of relief and thought to myself.....

"All had been restored."

Several years later, during the barley season, I watched as master negotiated the price of his crops with one of the sons of his most prosperous customer. The young man along with his servants brought livestock to trade—as far as the eye could see. He bargained hard with master, but in the end they happily shook hands.

"Ayala," master called out to me.

"Oh, how good it felt to finally be called by everyone the name my father had given me..... *Ayala*."

"Yes, my lord," I said, bowing.

After his illness, he often called for me. If it were possible for him to be any kinder than he already was, he still found unique ways to display his generosity towards me and mama. He took very good care of us.

"Stand up my child. You never have to do that again," he said. "You and your mother are family. I have four daughters instead of three," master said, laughing. "I do have something very important to share with you, Ayala. I suppose since you are like my eldest, I would like to offer you the privilege of marriage first. There is a young man that bargains hard with me from time to time. I'm sure you are aware of who I am speaking of. He has been coming here for several years now. Each time he arrives, and before he departs, he always asks about the fair maiden," he said, smiling. "He comes from a wealthy family who trusts God, Ayala. He is convinced after coming here these years, that you should be his wife." Master looked lovingly at me. "I believe you will be happy with this man."

Mistress and mama were over-joyed when I shared the news.

"I know the young man well," mistress said. "He is handsome and I also believe he will make a very fine husband."

Later that afternoon, I raced to my secret place to discuss the matter of the young man's proposal.

The area had always been special to me, but ever since the storm, it had become more than just a hiding place.

It was a place where I enjoyed talking to God.

***~

*1 He that dwelleth in the secret place of the most High shall abide under the shadow of the Almighty.*

*2 I will say of the LORD, He is my refuge and my fortress: my God; in him will I trust.*

*3 Surely he shall deliver thee from the snare of the fowler, and from the noisome pestilence.*

*4 He shall cover thee with his feathers, and under his wings shalt thou trust: his truth shall be thy shield and buckler.*

*5 Thou shalt not be afraid for the terror by night; nor for the arrow that flieth by day;*

*6 Nor for the pestilence that walketh in darkness; nor for the destruction that wasteth at noonday.*

*7 A thousand shall fall at thy side, and ten thousand at thy right hand; but it shall not come nigh thee.*

*8 Only with thine eyes shalt thou behold and see the reward of the wicked.*

*9 Because thou hast made the LORD, which is my refuge, even the most High, thy habitation;*

*10 There shall no evil befall thee, neither shall any plague come nigh thy dwelling.*

*11 For he shall give his angels charge over thee, to keep thee in all thy ways.*

*12 They shall bear thee up in their hands, lest thou dash thy foot against a stone.*

*13 Thou shalt tread upon the lion and adder: the young lion and the dragon shalt thou trample under feet.*

*14 Because he hath set his love upon me, therefore will I deliver him: I will set him on high, because he hath known my name.*

*15 He shall call upon me, and I will answer him: I will be with him in trouble; I will deliver him, and honour him.*

*16 With long life will I satisfy him, and shew him my salvation.*

(The Bible: King James Version)

# About the Author

**Rhonda Washington Nelson** is a fictional writer who loves telling stories of real life events with a spiritual context. Rhonda's faith is the foundation for all of her writings. Heavily influenced by her mother and grandmother, she loves telling stories that glorifies Jesus Christ. Rhonda is the author of "No Other Help I Know", "The Sensitivity Chip" and "A Believer's Guide to Witnessing". When she is not writing, she is President/CEO of The Washington Health Group and Kingdom Novels. Her primary goal and focus in life is based on the scripture given in Matthew 6:33…. "but seek ye first the kingdom of God and His righteousness, and all these things shall be added unto you."